W9-BPR-508

Five Nights at Freddy's™

SURVIVAL

~~SECURITY~~ LOGBOOK

Based on the series Five Nights at Freddy's, created by Scott Cawthon

Copyright © 2018 Scott Cawthon. All rights reserved.

All rights reserved. Published by Scholastic Inc., *Publishers since 1920.*
SCHOLASTIC and associated logos are trademarks and/or
registered trademarks of Scholastic Inc.

The publisher does not have any control over and does not assume any responsibility
for author or third-party websites or their content.

No part of this publication may be reproduced, stored in a retrieval system, or transmitted in any
form or by any means, electronic, mechanical, photocopying, recording, or otherwise, without written
permission of the publisher. For information regarding permission, write to Scholastic Inc.,
Attention: Permissions Department, 557 Broadway,
New York, NY 10012.

This book is a work of fiction. Names, characters, places, and incidents are either the product of the author's
imagination or are used fictitiously, and any resemblance to actual persons, living or dead,
business establishments, events, or locales is entirely coincidental.

Photos © Shutterstock: cover blood spots and throughout (Gl0ck);
cover brown texture (homydesign); cover beige texture (NataLT); 1 background and throughout (alexandre17);
2 center (Lyudmyla Kharlamova); 3 coffee ring and throughout (Africa Studio); 42 center (Alexandr III);
42 bottom left and right (olllikeballoon); 43 top (Ksenya Savva); 43 right (olllikeballoon); 43 bottom (Studio_G);
52 bottom (Lyudmyla Kharlamova); 64 tape and throughout (jocic).

ISBN 978-1-338-22930-1

10 9 8 7 6 5 4 3 2 1 18 19 20 21 22

Printed in the U.S.A. 88

First printing 2018
Art by Tina Francisco and Katrina Mae Hao
Book design by Carolyn Bull

THIS BOOK BELONGS TO:

~~MIKE~~

Sorry—looks like somebody's already written in this one . . . You don't mind, right?

HOW TO USE THIS LOGBOOK

Welcome to the first day of your exciting new career! This journal was designed for you, Fazbear Entertainment's newest employee, to both welcome you and ensure you feel fulfilled and prepared during your first week on the job. We don't want you to feel overwhelmed, otherwise you might not come back!

After each night's work, we ask that you take a moment for self-reflection by completing the various activities in the pages that follow. Some of these activities will review your training, while others will help you clear your mind and focus. And, of course, don't forget to log any strange events that occur throughout your shift.

Let's get started!

NIGHT 1: A THRILLING NEW CHAPTER!

To begin, we suggest you fill out some basic information in the unlikely event of an emergency. All set? Please cut out this contact card and return it to your supervisor at the end of your first shift.

Name: Owen

Phone: not telling

Address: not telling

Medications: none

Allergies: none

Organ Donor: NONE

End-of-Life Preferences:

age

In case of emergency, please contact:

Name: owen

Phone:

Relation:

Feeling down? Don't!

List ten reasons why applying to Freddy Fazbear's Pizza seemed like a good idea at the time.

1. Employees get free pizza.
2. _____
3. _____
4. _____
5. _____
6. _____
7. _____
8. _____
9. _____
10. _____

Would You Rather . . .

Hug Freddy? . . . or . . . Hug Foxy?

Work day shift with two parties? . . . or . . . Work night shift and clean up?

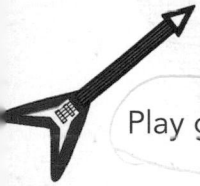

Play guitar with Bonnie? . . . or . . . Sing with Freddy?

Listen to Ballora's music all night? . . . or . . . Listen to the Puppet's music box all night?

Get an ice cream from Circus Baby? . . . or . . . Get a cupcake from Chica?

If you were going to design a new animatronic friend for the kids at one of Fazbear Entertainment's numerous enterprises, what would it look like? What special features might it have?

Special Features:

Quiz: Reviewing Your Training

Have you listened carefully to all the night guard training tapes? Test your knowledge here and see how you fared on page 12.

1. What's our motto at Freddy Fazbear's Pizza?

   a. A mystical place for kids and parents, where fantasy and intrigue come to light

   b. A magical place for kids and grown-ups alike, where fantasy and fun come to life

   c. A magnificent place for kids and grown-ups alike, where fun comes to life

2. Fazbear Entertainment is not responsible for damage to . . .

   a. Property or person

   b. Animatronics

   c. Kitchen equipment

3. Why are the animatronics left in free-roaming mode at night?

   a. There is no way to turn them off.

   b. They need to blow off some steam at the end of the day.

   c. Their servos lock up if they are turned off for too long.

4. If the animatronics see you after hours, they'll most likely believe you're . . .

a. A metal endoskeleton without its costume on

b. A security guard

c. A child in need of a hug

5. Why should you only close the doors and operate the lights/cameras when absolutely necessary?

a. We are currently involved in an "eco-friendly" initiative.

b. The building has limited power supply between 12 and 6 a.m.

c. The animatronics are drawn to the light.

6. Where are the most crucial blind spots in your cameras?

a. The kitchen

b. Outside Pirate Cove

c. Right outside the office doors

Quiz Results: How Did You Do?

Tally up your score!

1. Correct answer: b.
2. Correct answer: a.
3. Correct answer: c.
4. Correct answer: a.
5. Correct answer: b.
6. Correct answer: c.

2 or fewer correct answers

Are you sure this is the job for you? You made some serious errors in your responses. Please thoroughly review your training before returning tomorrow.

3–4 correct answers

Your answers were partially correct, but we recommend brushing up on some of your responsibilities before your next shift. After all, one mistake could have dire consequences.

5 or more correct answers

You have the best chances for ~~success in~~ SURVIVAL this position. Job well done!

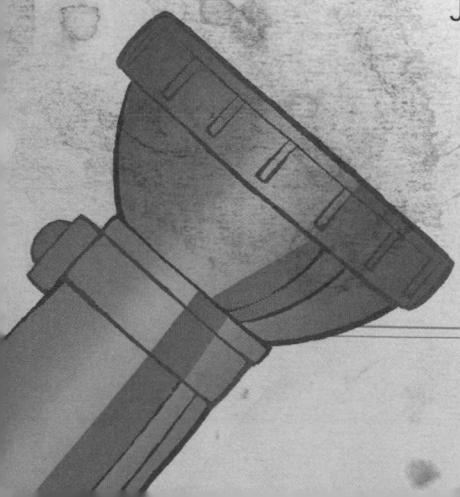

When you're scared, it can sometimes help to imagine what you fear in a funny way. Let's try it out—sketch and color in a silly costume for the Puppet to wear.

You know what they say—laugh and the world laughs with you. Cry and you cry alone. Make up some jokes for Freddy and his friends to make you laugh on the next page!

not FUNNY!!

HA! HA!!

Working the night shift can be hard, especially when the people closest to you work daylight hours. List the five people you most want to see at the end of the day.

1. _____

2. _____

3. _____

4. _____

5. _____

Who would you recommend for this job?

_____

_____

_____

_____

_____

_____

_____

_____

Take your family OUT . . .

for a night of fun at

Freddy Fazbear's Pizza!

Perfect Pizza Pack

Save $8!

Offer not valid when combined with other offers.

- TWO medium pizzas with your choice of TWO toppings each
- 15 game/ride tokens
- 1 pitcher of soda

FREDDY FAZBEAR'S PIZZA

Save $8!

Freddy's Fun Time

Save $5!

Offer not valid when combined with other offers.

- 30 game/ride tokens
- One large pizza with an additional topping
- 1 pitcher of soda

FREDDY FAZBEAR'S PIZZA

Save $5!

Foxy's Pirate-Palooza

Save $6!

Offer not valid when combined with other offers.

- Visit from Foxy at Pirate Cove
- 45 game/ride tokens
- 12 novelty eye patches

FREDDY FAZBEAR'S PIZZA

Save $6!

Make your workspace feel like home! What decorations can you add to your desk to make the space feel more cozy?

As a child, what did you want to be when you grew up? How does this differ from your current job prospects?

WHAT DO YOU REMEMBER?

Imagine that you've received a promising new opportunity to become a manager at a Freddy Fazbear's Pizza. It's up to you to make the big decisions that keep our customers coming back. Try making some of these decisions in the space below.

1. Would you make more human or animal animatronics?

_____

2. Would your animatronic friends be shiny and glossy, or soft and fuzzy?

_____

3. Which would you serve the most of—cupcakes, ice cream, or pizza?

_____

4. Would you give Circus Baby a hug if she gave you an ice cream cone?

_____

Make a bucket list of all the things you'd most like to do in life. What is holding you back from doing them? You never know how much time you have left!

1. _____

2. _____

3. _____

4. _____

5. _____

6. _____

7. _____

8. _____

9. _____

10. _____

After your first night on the job, we bet you're feeling pretty grateful to be alive. Reflect on the things in life that you are most thankful for.

WAS YOUR FAVORITE CHILDHOOD TOY A PLASTIC PURPLE TELEPHONE?

EVENT LOG: NIGHT 1

Please report any unusual events in the space below.

INCIDENT REPORT

Date: _____ Time: _____ a.m./p.m.

Night Guard on Duty: _____

Person(s) Involved: _____

Animatronic(s) Involved: _____

Description of Events: _____

_____

Injury ☐ Property Damage ☐ Death ☐

Missing Persons ☐ Police Involved ☐

Signature _____

INCIDENT REPORT

Date: _____ Time: _____ a.m./p.m.

Night Guard on Duty: _____

Person(s) Involved: _____

Animatronic(s) Involved: _____

Description of Events: _____

_____

Injury ☐ Property Damage ☐ Death ☐

Missing Persons ☐ Police Involved ☐

Signature _____

INCIDENT REPORT

Date: _____ Time: _____ a.m./p.m.

Night Guard on Duty: _____

Person(s) Involved: _____

Animatronic(s) Involved: _____

Description of Events: _____

_____

Injury ☐ Property Damage ☐ Death ☐

Missing Persons ☐ Police Involved ☐

Signature _____

Feelings About Tonight's Shift

Please circle how you would rate your feelings on a scale of 1–10, with 10 being the best, and 1 being the worst, on the scale below.

Overall:	1	2	3	4	5	6	7	8	9	10
Fulfillment:	1	2	3	4	5	6	7	8	9	10
Health:	1	2	3	4	5	6	7	8	9	10
Stress:	1	2	3	4	5	6	7	8	9	10
Purpose:	1	2	3	4	5	6	7	8	9	10
Hope:	1	2	3	4	5	6	7	8	9	10
Existential Dread:	1	2	3	4	5	6	7	8	9	10

NIGHT 2:

ANOTHER CHANCE TO SHINE!

Employment is vital to any well-functioning society.
List ten reasons why you really need this job.

1. _____

2. _____

3. _____

4. _____

5. _____

6. _____

7. _____

8. _____

9. _____

10. _____

If you were a child, what prizes would you want to see behind the prize counter? Draw them here.

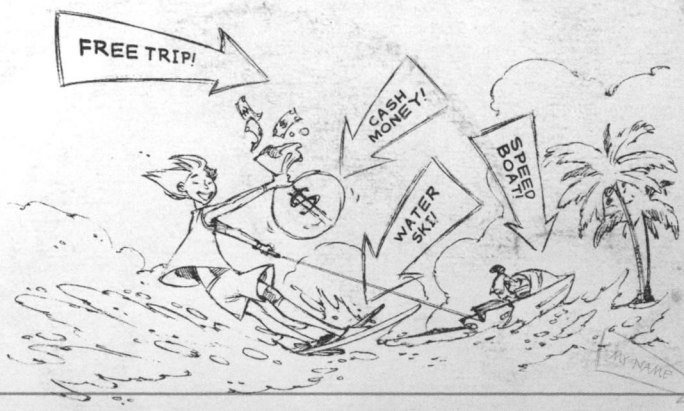
FREE TRIP!
CASH MONEY!
WATER SKI!
SPEED BOAT!

It's important to have heroes to aspire to. List your favorite characters from movies, books, and television who showed bravery in the face of extreme obstacles. Can you relate your current experiences to their heroic journeys?

Movies

Books

Television

Clara from "The Immortal and the Restless" because everything about this place is crazy and no one seems to notice except me.

Reflect on the happiest day of your life. Write about one specific memory from that day that will make you feel better if you find yourself facing new ~~difficulties.~~ CERTAIN DEATH!!

DO YOU REMEMBER YOUR NAME?

One way to find hope in a seemingly hopeless situation is to fast-forward and try peeking into the future. Let's give it a try—what will your life look like in five years?

Take a BITE . . .

out of fun

On your next birthday!

Chica's Cupcake Chaos

Save $4!

Offer not valid when combined with other offers.

- 12 cupcakes
- 20 game/ride tokens
- Custom Party Kit with invitations and hats

Save $4!

Birthday Ball

Save $6!

Offer not valid when combined with other offers.

- 24 balloons
- 20 game/ride tokens
- Custom Party Kit with invitations and hats

Save $6!

Happiest Day

Save $8!

Offer not valid when combined with other offers.

- Reserved Party Room
- Three-tier birthday cake
- Receive a gift from the Puppet
- Custom Party Kit with invitations and hats

Save $8!

To help you reach a more stable and relaxing frame of mind, write down your favorite **therapeutic musical** selections. Please note that some animatronics are audio-activated, so refrain from playing music in the workplace.

_____ / _____
(song) (artist)

_____ / _____
(song) (artist)

_____ / _____
(song) (artist)

_____ / _____
(song) (artist)

If you had to survive in a small crawl space under a desk for a week while surrounded by baby-themed animatronics, **would you rather . . .**

Sleep with one eye open? . . . or . . . Not sleep at all?

Eat only baked beans? . . . or . . . Eat only tuna salad?

Make a plan to escape? . . . or . . . Make a plan to call for help?

Listen to a creepy voice? . . . or . . . Listen to the silence?

Lose your frontal lobe? . . . or . . . Lose an arm?

Make an exercise schedule! Working out can keep your mind healthy, too, speeding up reaction times that are key to ~~success in~~ SURVIVAL your new position. Plan some activities for the week.

MONDAY

8 a.m. _____ 1 p.m. _____

9 a.m. _____ 2 p.m. _____

10 a.m. _____ 3 p.m. _____

11 a.m. _____ 4 p.m. _____

12 p.m. _____ 5 p.m. _____

TUESDAY

8 a.m. _____ 1 p.m. _____

9 a.m. _____ 2 p.m. _____

10 a.m. _____ 3 p.m. _____

11 a.m. _____ 4 p.m. _____

12 p.m. _____ 5 p.m. _____

WEDNESDAY

8 a.m. _____ 1 p.m. _____

9 a.m. _____ 2 p.m. _____

10 a.m. _____ 3 p.m. _____

11 a.m. _____ 4 p.m. _____

12 p.m. _____ 5 p.m. _____

THURSDAY

8 a.m. _____
9 a.m. _____
10 a.m. _____
11 a.m. _____
12 p.m. _____
1 p.m. _____
2 p.m. _____
3 p.m. _____
4 p.m. _____
5 p.m. _____

FRIDAY

8 a.m. _____
9 a.m. _____
10 a.m. _____
11 a.m. _____
12 p.m. _____
1 p.m. _____
2 p.m. _____
3 p.m. _____
4 p.m. _____
5 p.m. _____

SATURDAY

8 a.m. _____
9 a.m. _____
10 a.m. _____
11 a.m. _____
12 p.m. _____
1 p.m. _____
2 p.m. _____
3 p.m. _____
4 p.m. _____
5 p.m. _____

SUNDAY

8 a.m. _____
9 a.m. _____
10 a.m. _____
11 a.m. _____
12 p.m. _____
1 p.m. _____
2 p.m. _____
3 p.m. _____
4 p.m. _____
5 p.m. _____

Workout Suggestions

- Run five miles
- Run even faster
- Take a self-defense class

Think about some steps you can take to improve your productivity at work.

Step 1:

Step 2:

Step 3:

Helpful hint: Cutting down on distractions is key to noticing subtle changes in your environment. These subtle changes are often the forerunner of ~~security~~ threats.

animatronic

Draw yourself as an animatronic. What special abilities would you have?

Studies show that you forget half of your dreams in the first five minutes after waking. Use this page and the next page to sketch and write notes about your **recent dreams**. Reflect on the meaning of your dreams.

DO YOU HAVE DREAMS?

DO ANY OF THESE TOYS LOOK FAMILIAR TO YOU?

MY NAME
ONE OF THESE
BELONG TO YOU?

Story Starter: Where's Foxy?

Flex your creative muscles by writing your own short story in the space below. You can use this starting prompt to kick your imagination into high gear.

I checked the security cameras, cycling through the feeds until I came back to Pirate Cove once again. Where could Foxy be? Suddenly I heard a *thud, thud, thud,* like the heavy pounding of animatronic footsteps. I turned to my left, and . . .

EVENT LOG: NIGHT 2

Please report any unusual events in the space below.

INCIDENT REPORT

Date: _____ Time: _____ a.m./p.m.

Night Guard on Duty: _____

Person(s) Involved: _____

Animatronic(s) Involved: _____

Description of Events: _____

_____

Injury ☐ Property Damage ☐ Death ☐

Missing Persons ☐ Police Involved ☐

Signature _____

INCIDENT REPORT

Date: _____ Time: _____ a.m./p.m.

Night Guard on Duty: _____

Person(s) Involved: _____

Animatronic(s) Involved: _____

Description of Events: _____

_____

Injury ☐ Property Damage ☐ Death ☐

Missing Persons ☐ Police Involved ☐

Signature _____

INCIDENT REPORT

Date: _____ Time: _____ a.m./p.m.

Night Guard on Duty: _____

Person(s) Involved: _____

Animatronic(s) Involved: _____

Description of Events: _____

_____

Injury ☐ Property Damage ☐ Death ☐

Missing Persons ☐ Police Involved ☐

Signature _____

Feelings About Tonight's Shift

Please circle how you would rate your feelings on a scale of 1–10, with 10 being the best, and 1 being the worst, on the scale below.

Overall:	1	2	3	4	5	6	7	8	9	10
Fulfillment:	1	2	3	4	5	6	7	8	9	10
Health:	1	2	3	4	5	6	7	8	9	10
Stress:	1	2	3	4	5	6	7	8	9	10
Purpose:	1	2	3	4	5	6	7	8	9	10
Hope:	1	2	3	7	2	6	7	8	9	10
Existential Dread:	1	2	3	4	5	6	7	8	9	10

NIGHT 3:

NOW YOU'RE GETTING IT!

Welcome back to another pivotal night of your thriving new career, where you get to really ask yourself, "What am I doing with my life? What would my friends say?" And most importantly, "Will I ever see my family again?" **Let's get started by listing ten bad habits you'd like to break.**

1. Chewing gum excessively.
2. _____
3. _____
4. _____
5. _____
6. _____
7. _____
8. _____
9. _____
10. _____

Quiz: Operating Spring Lock Suits

Did you review the training tapes about our new spring lock suits? Remember: You must review this vital training before interacting with a spring lock suit/animatronic.

1. What makes a spring lock suit different from a standard animatronic?

   a. It can make ice cream and inflate balloons.

   b. It's more dangerous than the standard animatronic.

   c. It doubles as both an animatronic and a mascot costume.

2. While in animatronic mode, spring lock suits walk toward what?

   a. Light

   b. Sound

   c. Birthday cake

3. To recoil the animatronic parts, you must use which tool?

   a. A handcrank

   b. Your fingers

   c. A wrench

4. Which of the following should you not do to the spring locks?

a. Breathe on them

b. Touch them

c. All of the above

5. If you trip the spring locks, what should you do?

a. Die in front of customers

b. Scream for help

c. Head to an offstage area before bleeding out

6. Failing to follow the rules may result in what?

a. Firing

b. Accidents/injury/death/irreparable and grotesque maiming

c. Promotion

Quiz Results: How Did You Do?

Tally up your score!

1. Correct answer: c.
2. Correct answer: b.
3. Correct answer: a.
4. Correct answer: c.
5. Correct answer: c.
6. Correct answer: b.

2 or fewer correct answers

Please review your training before you even look at another spring lock suit, and *don't* speak to any insurance agents should you encounter them.

3–4 correct answers

You gave some half-right answers here. We recommend reviewing your training with the audiocassette tapes.

5 or more correct answers

You paid attention! You may not need to wear a spring lock suit as part of your night guard duties, but you know how to handle a spring lock animatronic if you encounter it.

Disregard this quiz—
in fact, don't mention the
spring lock suits to anyone.

Even the animatronics get stressed out sometimes. Imagine you were going to send the animatronics on vacation. Where would you send each one?

Freddy: _____

Why: _____

_____

Chica: _____

Why: _____

_____

Bonnie: _____

Why: _____

_____

Foxy: _____

Why: _____

_____

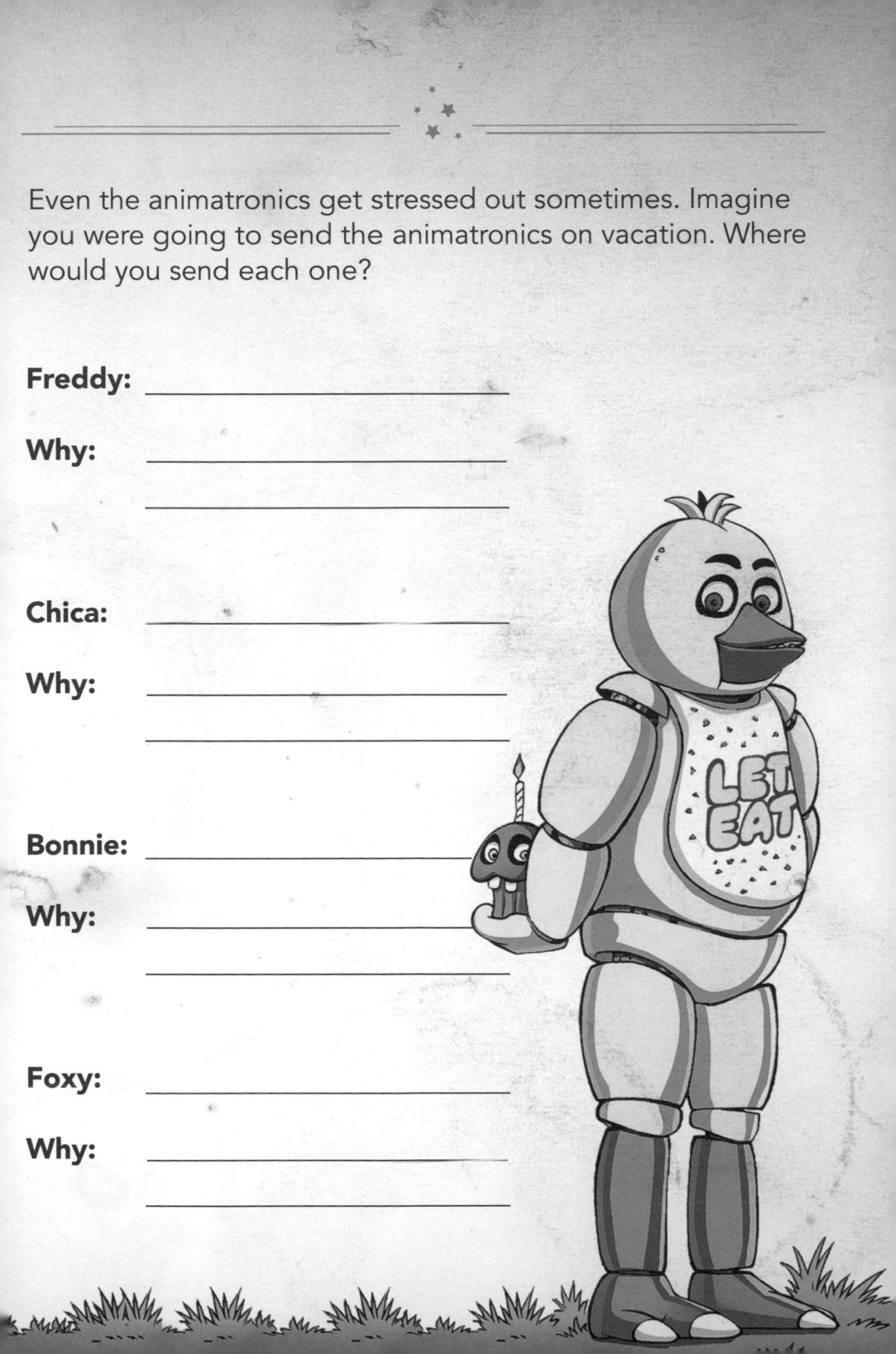

During your first week on the job, it can be hard to keep the rules straight, so we've made you this handy checklist!

+ DO follow custom rules for specified animatronics
+ DO listen carefully for new/unfamiliar sounds
+ DO monitor systems and animatronics as necessary
+ DO avoid the animatronics to the best of your ability

- DON'T stare at the camera feeds for too long
- DON'T admit any prior employees

Design a new and advanced endoskeleton.

List some things that would be great to have in a pizzeria that would distract people from the depressing realities of life.

WAS YOUR FAVORITE RIDE THE CAROUSEL?

Create a new game for kids to play with Ballora.
Remember, Ballora inspires kids to get fit and enjoy pizza!

How to Play:

Word Search

See if you can spot all the Fazbear Entertainment–related words in the jumble below!

I T S M S E I T S M E I G T W
S M E I C T S M E I T S U M H
E I C T I S M E I T S M A E O
I T A S T M P L A Y E I R T A
S M K E O I T F O X Y S D M R
E I E T B S M E I T B S M E E
L I T S O M E I T S O M E I Y
E T S M R E I T S M N E I T O
T S A M N E I T S M N E I T U
S S Z M O E F I C H I C A T S
E M Z E T I U Y D D E R F T S
A M I E F I N T S M E I T S M
T E P I A T S M E I P A R T Y
T S M E L A U G H I T S M E I
W H A T I S Y O U R N A M E T

Afton Robotics Chica Party Foxy
Freddy Bonnie Let's Eat Pizza Laugh
Fun Cake Guard Play

WHAT DO YOU SEE?

If the animatronics could talk, what do you think they would say?

Use the comic panels below to illustrate your own comic about Freddy and Foxy.

FRIDAY

5+4
3

Fazbear Entertainment is often looking to rebrand whenever a PR disaster strikes.
Use the space below to design a new logo!

SLICE . . .

up some family fun at

Freddy Fazbear's Pizza!

ve
4!

Bonnie's Blast

Save
$4!

Offer not valid when combined with other offers.

FREDDY FAZBEAR'S PIZZA

- 15 game/ride tokens
- One large pizza with an additional topping
- 1 pitcher of soda

ve
4!

Save
$4!

ve
5!

Hungry Fazbear

Save
$5!

Offer not valid when combined with other offers.

FREDDY FAZBEAR'S PIZZA

- Two large pizzas with an additional topping
- 2 pitchers of soda
- 4 cupcakes

ve
5!

Save
$5!

ve
6!

Party Time!

Save
$6!

Offer not valid when combined with other offers.

FREDDY FAZBEAR'S PIZZA

- 30 game/ride tokens
- Two large pizzas with an additional topping
- 1 pitcher of soda

ve
6!

Save
$6!

You're part of the Fazbear family now! Draw yourself into the photos below.

EVENT LOG: NIGHT 3

Please report any unusual events in the space below.

INCIDENT REPORT

Date: _____ Time: _____ a.m./p.m.

Night Guard on Duty: _____

Person(s) Involved: _____

Animatronic(s) Involved: _____

Description of Events: _____

_____

Injury ☐ Property Damage ☐ Death ☐

Missing Persons ☐ Police Involved ☐

Signature _____

INCIDENT REPORT

Date: _____ Time: _____ a.m./p.m.

Night Guard on Duty: _____

Person(s) Involved: _____

Animatronic(s) Involved: _____

Description of Events: _____

_____

Injury ☐ Property Damage ☐ Death ☐

Missing Persons ☐ Police Involved ☐

Signature _____

INCIDENT REPORT

Date: _____ Time: _____ a.m./p.m.

Night Guard on Duty: _____

Person(s) Involved: _____

Animatronic(s) Involved: _____

Description of Events: _____

_____

Injury ☐ Property Damage ☐ Death ☐

Missing Persons ☐ Police Involved ☐

Signature _____

Feelings About Tonight's Shift

Please circle how you would rate your feelings on a scale of 1–10, with 10 being the best, and 1 being the worst, on the scale below.

Overall:	1	2	3	4	5	6	7	8	9	10
Fulfillment:	1	2	3	4	5	6	7	8	9	10
Health:	1	2	3	4	5	6	7	8	9	10
Stress:	1	2	3	4	5	6	7	8	9	10
Purpose:	1	2	3	4	5	6	7	8	9	10
Hope:	1	2	3	4	5	6	7	8	9	10
Existential Dread:	1	2	3	4	5	6	7	8	9	10

NIGHT 4:

WHAT ARE YOU STILL DOING HERE?

What are some poor decisions made by previous security guards that you will not repeat?

1. _____

2. _____

3. _____

4. _____

5. _____

6. _____

7. _____

8. _____

9. _____

10. _____

If you were to die in a grisly work accident—for instance, being stuffed inside an animatronic suit—who are the people you would miss the most?

DO YOU MISS THEM?

Write a personal message to each person describing how you met your terrible end, including the animatronic that got you.

Dear _____

_____

_____

_____

_____

_____

Dear _____

_____

_____

_____

_____

_____

Dear _____

_____

_____

_____

_____

_____

Think up an arcade game based on the adventures of the animatronics! Will Foxy sail the seven seas, or will Chica bake a cupcake fit for a king? Write about it here, and then draw a prototype arcade machine.

Game Title: _____

Description: _____

_____

_____

_____

Draw two screenshots from your game!

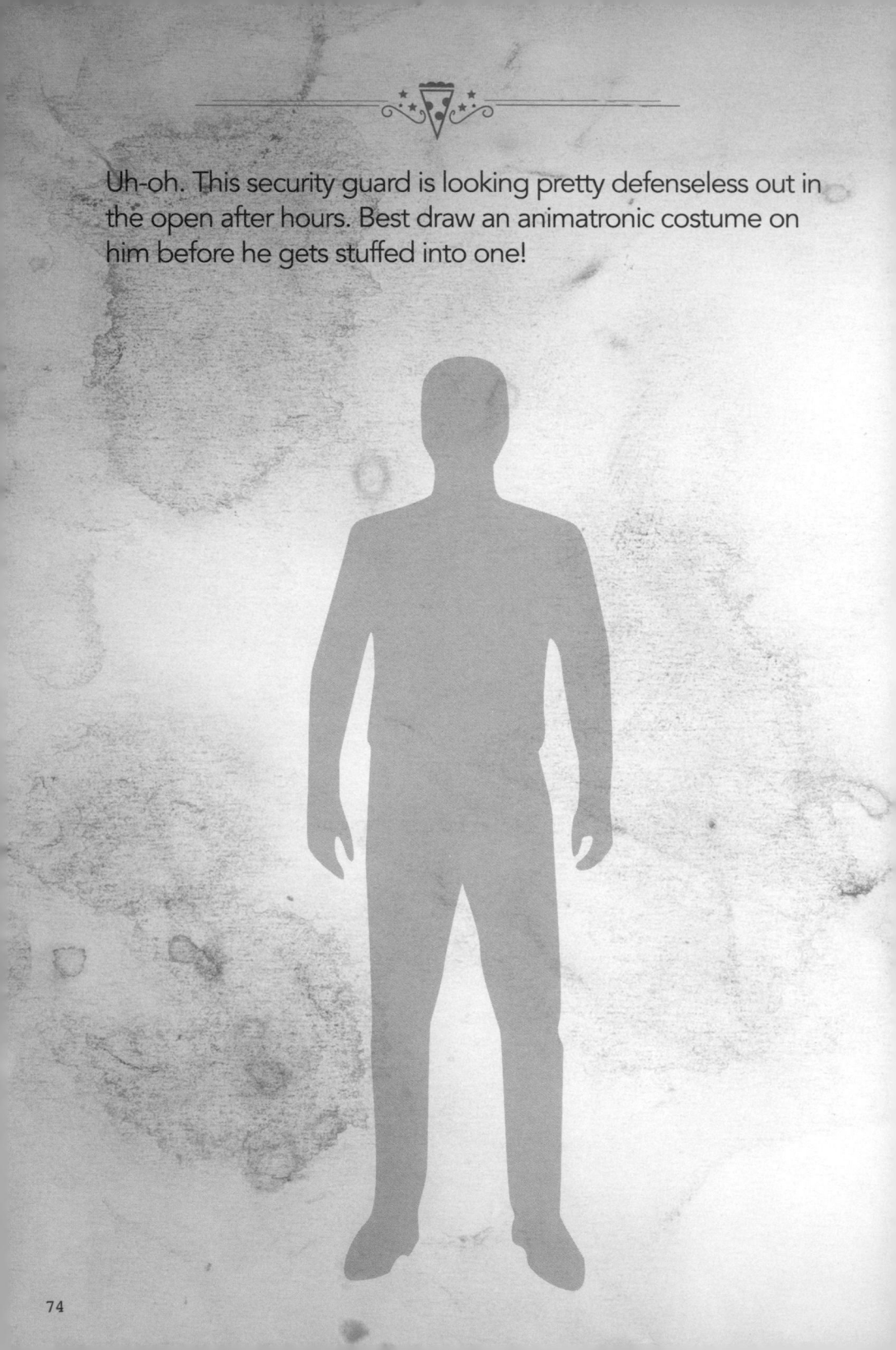

Uh-oh. This security guard is looking pretty defenseless out in the open after hours. Best draw an animatronic costume on him before he gets stuffed into one!

In the face of extreme fear, it can be calming to think back to your childhood. Did you have a stuffed animal or blanket that you took with you everywhere? What about an imaginary friend? Write about them here.

DOES HE STILL TALK TO YOU?

Quiz: Unlocking Your Potential

Now that you've gotten your bearings, it's time to really test your knowledge. Let's see if you've mastered the job!

1. Over time, you've learned that it's perhaps most important to . . .

   a. Scream when an animatronic approaches.

   b. Make loud noises.

   c. Watch the video feeds.

2. When you hear clanking in the kitchen, it's probably . . .

   a. Foxy

   b. Bonnie

   c. Chica

3. Freddy and his friends tend to become more active . . .

   a. If you check the cameras more often

   b. As the week progresses

   c. If you close the doors

4. Foxy and Bonnie tend to stick to the left side of the restaurant, while Chica and Freddy typically approach from . . .

   a. The right side of the restaurant

   b. Behind you

   c. The left side of the restaurant

5. In general, if you hallucinate seeing strange animatronics while on the job, it's best to . . .

   a. Take a good look at them.

   b. Abandon all hope.

   c. Bring up your video feeds.

6. If you do encounter an animatronic, it's best to refrain from . . .

   a. Making eye contact

   b. Doing a dance

   c. Running away screaming

Quiz Results: How Did You Do?

Tally up your score!

1. Correct answer: c.
2. Correct answer: c.
3. Correct answer: b.
4. Correct answer: a.
5. Correct answer: c.
6. Correct answer: a.

2 or fewer correct answers

Uh-oh. Looks like you've got quite a way to go before you've mastered your duties. You might just need more on-the-job experience, but we're afraid the learning curve is quite steep. Still, we hope you make it long enough to improve!

3–4 correct answers

You're getting there! You may have made a few mistakes in your answers, but it looks like you're starting to catch on.

5 or more correct answers

Wow! While we admit that a person in this unskilled position is usually considered expendable, we're very impressed with how quickly you've mastered your night guard responsibilities. Well done!

GRAND REOPENING!

Join us at the new

Freddy Fazbear's Pizza!

ave
12!

Offer not valid when combined with other offers.

Bonnie's New Groove

FREDDY FAZBEAR'S PIZZA

Save
$12!

- Special dance party with the animatronics
- Two large pizzas with an additional topping

ave
12!

Save
$12!

ave
14!

Offer not valid when combined with other offers.

Freddy's Fancy

FREDDY FAZBEAR'S PIZZA

Save
$14!

- 12 bow ties
- TWO large pizzas with TWO additional toppings
- Two pitchers of soda

ave
14!

Save
$14!

ave
16!

Offer not valid when combined with other offers.

Pizza Party Pack

FREDDY FAZBEAR'S PIZZA

Save
$16!

- Three large pizzas, each with an additional topping
- Three pitchers of soda
- 24 cupcakes

For real value, see page 61

ave
16!

Save
$16!

Switching to the Day Shift

Flex your creative muscles by writing your own short story in the space below. You can use this starting prompt to kick your imagination into high gear.

I'd only been on night shift for about a week, but I was so relieved to be switched over to the day shift. There's a lot of stress working 12 a.m.–6 a.m. My boss had told me that the animatronics were acting strangely—almost aggressive toward the staff—but I wasn't about to let that scare me off. After work I had an unsettling feeling that I was being followed home . . .

Keep the creativity going by writing a new song for Freddy and his friends to perform.

Now that you have the song down, draw the animatronics moving to the beat!

IS THIS SONG FAMILIAR TO YOU?

Can you navigate the maze below to get to the safe room?

START

Show Stage

Parts/
Service

Kitchen

FINISH

MY NAME

Freddy Fazbear's Pizza is committed to family fun, and above all—**safety!** By now we're sure you have our Rules for Safety memorized, but are there any that you would add to the list?

RULES FOR SAFETY

1. Don't run.
2. Don't yell.
3. Don't scream.
4. Don't poop on floor.
5. Stay close to mom.
6. Don't touch Freddy.
7. Don't hit.
8. Leave before dark.
9. _____
10. _____
11. _____
12. _____
13. _____
14. _____
15. _____

thank you,
management.

Who Would Win?

If the animatronics were battling for control of the pizzeria, who do you think would win and why?

VS.

Winner: _____

_____

_____

VS.

Winner: _____

_____

_____

VS.

Winner: _____

_____

_____

VS.

Winner: _____

_____

_____

VS.

Winner: _____

_____

_____

For the glory of pizza!

EVENT LOG: NIGHT 4

Please report any unusual events in the space below.

INCIDENT REPORT

Date: _____ Time: _____ a.m./p.m.

Night Guard on Duty: _____

Person(s) Involved: _____

Animatronic(s) Involved: _____

Description of Events: _____

_____

Injury ☐ Property Damage ☐ Death ☐

Missing Persons ☐ Police Involved ☐

Signature _____

INCIDENT REPORT

Date: _____ Time: _____ a.m./p.m.

Night Guard on Duty: _____

Person(s) Involved: _____

Animatronic(s) Involved: _____

Description of Events: _____

_____

Injury ☐ Property Damage ☐ Death ☐

Missing Persons ☐ Police Involved ☐

Signature _____

INCIDENT REPORT

Date: _____ Time: _____ a.m./p.m.

Night Guard on Duty: _____

Person(s) Involved: _____

Animatronic(s) Involved: _____

Description of Events: _____

_____

Injury ☐ Property Damage ☐ Death ☐

Missing Persons ☐ Police Involved ☐

Signature _____

Feelings About Tonight's Shift

Please circle how you would rate your feelings on a scale of 1–10, with 10 being the best, and 1 being the worst, on the scale below.

Overall:	1	2	3	4	5	6	7	8	9	10
Fulfillment:	1	2	3	4	5	6	7	8	9	10
I can hear sounds:	1	2	3	4	5	6	7	8	9	10
Stress:	1	2	3	4	5	6	7	8	9	10
Purpose:	1	2	3	4	5	6	7	8	9	10
Hope:	1	2	3	4	5	6	7	8	9	10
It was for me:	1	2	3	4	5	6	7	8	9	10

NIGHT 5:
CONGRATULATIONS!
FREDDY FAZBEAR'S PIZZA
SECURITY

Welcome back to your last day on the job!
That is, the last day of your first week!
We can't believe you've made it this far—
what would it take to get you to come back next week?

You've earned your one-week bonus, which will be given to you in the form of a delightful gift basket, the cost of which will be taken out of your next paycheck. Design the gift basket you would like to receive in the space below.

If you had one piece of advice to give to the next night guard, what would it be?

Would You Rather . . .

Dance with Ballora? . . . or . . . Sing with Circus Baby?

Spend all night in a
spring lock suit? . . . or . . . Spend all night in the dark?

Perform maintenance
on Funtime Freddy? . . . or . . . Try to fix Mangle?

Win a prize from the
Get a gift from the Puppet? . . . or . . . prize counter?

Try to outrun the Puppet? . . . or . . . Try to outrun Foxy?

Here at Freddy Fazbear's Pizza, many of our arcade machines use 8-bit graphics.
Use the grids below to convert Foxy into an 8-bit graphic!

Let's Eat!

Design an elaborate birthday cake for our patrons. Detail the ingredients and steps to prepare it on the recipe card on these pages. Then draw your design.

Procedure

1. _____
_____
_____

2. _____
_____
_____

3. _____
_____
_____

4. _____
_____
_____

Draw your dish here.

Draw a birthday-themed animatronic worthy of delivering your new birthday cake in the space below.

When a PR disaster strikes, it's always good to have a plan. Think of alternate explanations to these common misunderstandings.

"My child said Freddy bit him!"

He tripped and fell on Freddy's teeth. Not our fault.

"That animatronic is filthy and oozing liquid!"

"My child went missing in your pizzeria!"

"My pizza has mold on it."

Pretend you're an architect and imagine the optimal layout for a Freddy Fazbear's Pizza. Draw it here.

To celebrate the end of your first week, plan a party! You can use the space below to get it organized.

Theme

Where

When

Decorations

Menu

People to Invite

THE PARTY WAS FOR YOU

Create a newspaper article all about the life and accomplishments of a heroic security guard who perished in the line of duty, defending the pizzeria and its guests.

HEROIC SECURITY GUARD DEFENDS FUN FOR ALL

Draw or paste an image of yourself here.

Draw all of your most valued treasures in the space below. Whom would you give each object to if you had to give them up?*

*Bonus: Consider seeking legal counsel to turn this list into a living will.

EVENT LOG: NIGHT 5

Please report any unusual events in the space below.

MY NAME

INCIDENT REPORT

Date: _____ Time: _____ a.m./p.m.

Night Guard on Duty: _____

Person(s) Involved: _____

Animatronic(s) Involved: _____

Description of Events: _____

_____

Injury ☐ Property Damage ☐ Death ☐

Missing Persons ☐ Police Involved ☐

Signature _____

INCIDENT REPORT

Date: _____ Time: _____ a.m./p.m.

Night Guard on Duty: _____

Person(s) Involved: _____

Animatronic(s) Involved: _____

Description of Events: _____

_____

Injury ☐ Property Damage ☐ Death ☐

Missing Persons ☐ Police Involved ☐

Signature _____

INCIDENT REPORT

Date: _____ Time: 8:11 a.m./p.m.

Night Guard on Duty: _____

Person(s) Involved: _____

Animatronic(s) Involved: _____

Description of Events: _____

_____

Injury ☐ Property Damage ☐ Death ☐

Missing Persons ☐ Police Involved ☐

Signature _____

Feelings About Tonight's Shift

Please circle how you would rate your feelings on a scale of 1–10, with 10 being the best, and 1 being the worst, on the scale below.

Overall:	1	2	3	4	5	6	7	8	9	10
I can't see:	1	2	3	4	5	6	7	8	9	10
Health:	1	2	3	4	5	6	7	8	9	10
Stress:	1	2	3	4	5	6	7	8	9	10
I'm scared:	1	2	3	4	5	6	7	8	9	10
Hope:	1	2	3	4	5	6	7	8	9	10
Existential Dread:	1	2	3	4	5	6	7	8	9	10

SEE YOU NEXT WEEK!

We at Fazbear Entertainment would like to thank you for joining our company. We hope this logbook helped you get a better handle on your responsibilities and also provided a bit of fun for you at the end of a long shift.

It's no small feat to survive the daily grind here, and we commend you for your courage and lack of common sense.

Until next time!